Foreword

I grew up in the days when the cinema was king. In the immediate post-war years 20 million film-goers went to the 'pictures' every week. They queued up outside the Odeons, the Granadas and ABCs, as well as outside such exotically named local cinemas as the Zonita, the Cosy or the Empire. It took only five decades for the cinema to develop into the biggest provider of mass entertainment which the world had ever known. But within a decade after the post-war relaunch of television the small screen was supreme. The mass cinema audience preferred to stay at home to watch BBC or ITV programmes rather than to dress up and turn out to go to the local cinema or 'fleapit' as they were often affectionately called.

I am pleased therefore to welcome George Peck's book on Bedfordshire Cinemas. It records the rise and fall of the cinema in the County and it tells the story of each individual picture-house with photographs and other interesting illustrations. He has managed to date precisely the opening and closing of most of the cinemas, and that in itself should settle many arguments! Moreover he has managed to talk to a number of cinema owners, managers and projectionists and has woven their memories into his narrative histories.

I am sure that for many readers this will be a most nostalgic book. It will bring back a host of memories, of long-forgotten films, of family outings, of courting in the back row and of the film stars who week by week caused us to pay our shillings and to be captured for two to three hours by the silver screen.

Mr Peck's book is a pioneer study of an aspect of recent history and I trust that it may help to bring to light other photographs and memorabilia of the cinema. I hope also that it will encourage other historians of the cinema to publish their histories.

C. Muris
County Librarian

Introduction

The material for this book has been collected over several years in order to record, in some lasting form, the heyday of the cinema. The aim has been to cover permanent buildings only, largely ignoring temporary cinemas in village halls. Most of the village halls in Bedfordshire have been licensed to show films at one time or another.

Major sources of information have been local newspapers held by the County Library in Bedford and Luton. Other information has been obtained from individuals, some of whom responded to letters published in the local press. The archives of the County Council proved useful for dating many cinemas and providing details of structures and equipment.

It is hoped that the present publication will provide a readable survey of its subject and encourage others to embark on further local research to reveal more close-up shots of the cinema in Bedfordshire.

G. C. Peck

Acknowledgements

The author wishes to acknowledge the help given to him by the past and present editors of the *Bedfordshire Times, Beds and Bucks Observer, Biggleswade Chronicle, Dunstable Gazette,* and the *Luton News.* The Eastern Arts Association has been helpful in tracing and providing illustrations.

The following have been very helpful by providing photographs and information:

Mr B. Albon who helped me with the Arlesey Cinemas.
Mr D. Bidwell who gave his permission for the use of the Ampthill photographs.
Mr L. W. Griffin who recalled memories of the Leighton Buzzard cinemas.
Mrs B. E. Rawlins who gave up an afternoon to talk about the Bedford cinemas.
Mr Smith whose family owned the Stotfold library – and lastly
Mr J. D. Squires who corrected some technical items for me.

Their help is gratefully acknowledged, as is that given by many members of the public who have written to the author about the early cinemas.

ISBN 0 901051 92 6
Published 1981
© Copyright Bedfordshire County Council
Printed by White Crescent Press Limited, Luton, Beds.

Photographs

I   The Picturedrome, Ampthill
II   The Electric Kinema, Ampthill
III   The Zonita, Ampthill
IV   The Cosy, Arlesey
V   Association Hall, Bedford
VI   The Empire, Bedford
VII   The Palace, Bedford
VIII   The Picturedrome, Bedford
IX   The Plaza, Bedford
X   The Empire, Biggleswade
XI   George's Hall, Biggleswade
XII   The Regal, Biggleswade
XIII   The Palace, Dunstable
XIV   The Union, Dunstable
XV   The Exchange, Leighton Buzzard
XVI   The Alma, Luton
XVII   The Empire, Luton
XVIII   The Anglo American Electric Picture Palace, Luton.
XIX   The Picturedrome, Luton
XX   The Savoy, Luton
XXI   The Union, Luton
XXII   The Parish Room, Potton, formerly Randall's Cinema.
XXIII   The Victory, Sandy
XXIV   Harold Ramsey. The Regent Cinema, Stotfold.
XXV   The Picturedrome, Toddington, later renamed The Cozy.
XXVI   Beds & Herts Pictorial, 1 August 1933

Many newspaper advertisements for cinema programmes are also included.

Part one

Introduction

The early film industry in the USA

The American film industry can be said to have begun when Thomas Edison developed his Kinetoscope peepshow machine, so providing the first way of exploiting the new invention of motion pictures. Kinetoscope parlours sprang up across America and machines were imported into Europe. The first films were made in the 'Black Maria' studio at West Grange, New Jersey and were 50 feet long, featuring vaudeville acts of the day. American films soon faced strong competition from films made in Europe, especially those made by the Lumière brothers in France and Robert Paul in Britain. Their films seemed more attractive because they had developed a portable camera which could take outdoor scenes from all over the world, unlike the Kinetoscope which could only be used in the 'Black Maria'. Films reached the American public as short interludes in the Vaudeville Theatres or as novelties shown by travelling showmen. When interest in the early films declined the public were attracted back by the innovations of Edwin S. Porter who was appointed by Edison to run his studios in 1900.

When longer films began to appear 'Nickelodeons' opened across America. Usually housed in the poorer districts of cities they charged 5 or 10 cents entrance money to see a programme of 5 or 6 films, the programme changing every few days. This era ended when more opulent theatres opened about 1917. Nickelodeons had a rival in Bioscope theatres. Bioscope cameras had been invented in France about 1891 by Georges Demeney. In 1892–3 he attempted to combine moving pictures with sound and had some success. This was not followed up until about 1926.

Thomas Edison had originally intended to synchronise the Kinetoscope with the phonograph to provide talking pictures. The first experiments used synchronised discs but were not too successful. It was not until *The Jazz Singer* appeared in 1927 that a demand for a system of recording sound on films was established. 'Western Electric' were early pioneers of what was to become the standard system.

The film industry in Britain and Europe

Robert Paul, a scientific instrument maker, was asked to copy the Kinetoscope machine in England to meet a local demand. He found that the machine was not patented outside America and within months had made his own camera which used the intermittent principle in the projector. This was demonstrated late in 1895. He and his partner, Birt Acres, produced their first film in 1895. Birt Acres filmed the Derby and the Boat Race the same year. In 1899 Paul opened the first film studios in Britain at Muswell Hill in North London where he produced a series of trick films.

Edison's Kinetoscope inspired the Lumière brothers in France to make projectors and cameras. Their system, the Cinematograph, was perfected in Paris. The brothers were the first to exploit the invention by distributing and producing films when they sent camera showmen on tours of Europe and Asia photographing, developing, and exhibiting films as they went.

In an attempt to control the expanding industry in Britain the Cinematograph Act of 1909 came into force. Public concern of the dangers of the inflammable film began with the Paris Charity Bazaar fire of 1897 when nearly 180 people died. Cinemas now had to be licensed by the local authority, with stringent conditions for handling the film and for the safety of the audience. Indirectly, the Act gave the local authority the power to censor the films shown. In 1912 the Kinematograph Manufacturers Association attempted to create order out of a potentially chaotic situation by setting up the British Board of Film Censors to provide self-censorship.

During the 1914–18 War the British, French, German and other film industries suffered a serious setback. The Americans were quick to exploit the situation and the myth of the American star was imprinted on the minds of British audiences to ensure a steady market. In 1921 the British National Film League tried to bolster the popularity and prestige of British films with special feature weeks throughout England but found that there were not enough good British films. The situation did not improve until the Cinematograph Act of 1927 imposed a quota system on renters and exhibitors. This guaranteed a showing and a reasonable financial return for British films.

By 1936 the two largest cinema groups were Gaumont-British and the Associated British Picture Corporation, who each owned about 300 cinemas out of the 4,400 in Britain. Other groups were to combine to form the Odeon Group backed by a wealthy Yorkshire flour miller, J. Arthur Rank. He had aimed to make religious films but difficulties arose that diverted him into joining General Film Distributors. In 1940 Gaumont-British was in financial collapse so Rank was able to purchase a majority holding. He later bought the Odeon circuit; the Denham studios which had aimed to rival Hollywood, Pinewood and the Gaumont-British Studios at Shepherd's Bush and Islington.

The cinema in neighbouring counties

The history of the cinema in Buckinghamshire, Hertfordshire and Northamptonshire parallels that of Bedfordshire. Films were first shown in village halls at Welwyn, Hertfordshire, but there was a spate of cinemas being opened in the period 1910–12 when Northampton saw the County Electric Pavilion and also King's Picture Palace being opened. Cheshunt in Hertfordshire also had a Palace opened in 1912, by which time Northampton had 5 cinemas and 2 theatres. Wollaston in Northamptonshire had a cinema set up in a second-hand ex-army hut with ill-fitting doors and windows that was so cold in winter that customers took cocoa tins stuffed with smouldering rags to warm their hands and feet.

The history of the cinema in these counties is that of rivalry between the cinemas and live theatres in the early years, and the cinema, television and bingo after the Second World War, as it was in Bedfordshire.

The early cinema in Bedfordshire

For many years at the beginning of the century the people of Bedfordshire had to watch the new-style entertainment in village halls, barns or in portable theatres. Their interest in moving pictures had been aroused by fairground entertainments such as 'dioramas' which were models that were lit from differing angles to get the effects. 'Dyson's Dioramas' and gypsy choir performed at the Corn Exchange in Bedford on the 14 May 1894, giving a children's performance at 5 pm that day and an adult show at 8 pm at which the diorama *Switzerland* was featured. The following day's show featured *Old Ireland*. Dyson's also appeared in Luton.

To regulate the growing industry parliament passed the Cinematograph Act 1909. This made the County Council responsible for controlling the cinema industry in Bedfordshire, and for ensuring that public safety measures were observed. Cinemas were, and are, inspected annually to see if repairs to the cinema have been done, fire precaution measures kept up to date, and the measures for the welfare of children observed. These duties Bedfordshire County Council delegated to a Stage Plays Performance Committee that had been set up in 1899.

Portable theatres were licensed by the Stage Plays Performance Committee to show films for limited periods in villages. These were hand-cranked 'animatograph' films. One man (William H. P. Weight – late Middlesex Regiment, RNAS, RAF) applied for an annual licence for his portable theatre that he intended to erect on the

Cock Inn meadow, Wootton as late as 1927. He claimed that he had been granted one by many authorities in the area. His theatre had tip-up seats for the 300 patrons and a wooden floor throughout; and there was lavatory accommodation provided. He also claimed that the theatre could be emptied in one minute in an emergency through the 7 exits (all of which opened outwards). The theatre was lit by a Thorn and Hoddle Patent safety acetylene plant. A plentiful supply of fire extinguishers, water buckets, and sand buckets were available. He had been in Arlesey the previous year and had a rival in George Allen who went to Harrold and Shefford with his portable theatre business.

The Blake brothers of Bedford were also local pioneers of the business taking their gas-illuminated projector to the villages in a pony and trap to show their animated photographs. The first show was apparently put on in the old schoolroom at Haynes. Their takings being £1 18s 10d, out of which they paid 4s for the hire of the hall and stabling for the pony.

William Norman Blake was born in 1871 and educated in Bedford. He became the acknowledged head of the industry in Bedfordshire and neighbouring counties. It is said that he took some of the earliest animated photographs ever made in England for which he received recognition at leading exhibitions in this country. William Blake became the President of the Cinematograph Association in 1926–7. He died in 1934.

His younger brother was Ernest Edgar Blake born in 1879 and died aged 82 in 1961. He joined his father's photographic business after leaving Bedford Modern School. Before entering the picture-making industry with Kodak.

In the earlier years of their enterprise they used projectors made by Lumière, Paul, Wrench and others. By the turn of the century they had a promising travelling show using gas-illuminated projectors. These trips produced many interesting anecdotes one of which involved another local pioneer Robert Chetham. The brothers were giving a programme in aid of the Biggleswade Volunteer Fire Brigade and one of the films showed the funeral of Queen Victoria. The sound of guns going off in salute to the dead Queen was made by someone hitting a gong held by Robert Chetham. Unfortunately the striker missed on one occasion and hit Chetham's hand causing him to drop the gong so knocking over the screen on to the front row of the audience! At about the same time they were asked to go to Thurleigh by the Vicar, Reverend Benjamin Trapp, to give a show in the schoolroom. The programme was mainly comic pictures (one featured a fight between a miller and a sweep) but there was also a feature concerning soldiers on the march which intrigued the audience. By way of a change local men sang songs during intervals between films. The schoolroom was so packed that the stage had to be taken down. A barn at Grove House Farm, Biddenham, was also used by the Blakes; here Robert Chetham sang songs to his own banjo accompaniment.

As well as running the cinemas in the Association Hall, Bedford, at the Picturedrome, the Palace, and the Empire in Bedford, the Blakes had two cinemas in Hitchin. Ernest Blake also had an interest in the Granada.

Charles Thurston, the fairground proprietor, exhibited films as part of his fair on Biggleswade Market Square. On one occasion he found a rival had established a wood and canvas theatre in the town so taking away his trade.

This makeshift period began to change as permanent buildings began to be adapted. In Bedford the *Chequers* public house was turned into the Palace Cinema in 1911, while in Ampthill the Salvation Army Barracks became the Picturedrome, and in Luton a disused propellor factory became the Empire. New cinemas in towns throughout Bedfordshire were built in the 1930s though occasional film shows in village halls continued for many years.

Topics of concern

Two topics have been of concern to the authorities over the years – the admission of children, and Sunday opening of cinemas.

Bedford can be taken as an example of the events leading to Sunday opening of cinemas. In November 1939 the officer commanding a military unit in Bedford wrote to the Town Clerk asking for the cinemas to be opened between 4pm and 10 pm on Sundays. The town Clerk explained the necessary procedures that would have to be taken by the Borough Council before they could apply to the Home Secretary for an order allowing cinemas to be opened. The Council was required to organise a poll of electors in order to test their feelings, if this was requested by 100 electors. One was demanded and this resulted in approximately one-eighth of the electors voting: 1627 voted against opening and 1444 voting in favour. No further action was taken at that time. However, the Air Officer in charge of Balloon Command, RAF, pursued the matter and the Watch Committee decided to consider the matter further. The Army Commanding Officer, East Anglian Area wrote in support of his RAF colleagues in

January 1940, but the Methodist Churches in the area and the Bedford Sunday Defence Committee objected causing the Watch Committee to refer the matter to the full Council. They decided to submit a request to the Home Office for a Draft order giving the necessary authority to open on Sundays. Parliament agreed to the Sunday opening of cinemas in Bedford in March 1940. The County Council gave their approval in the same month for the whole of the county.

The admission of children to cinemas was of concern, because many felt that if young children attended the cinema they would absorb and adopt an attitude to life which would not improve their social conduct. In May 1945 the Dean of St Albans wrote to the Town Clerk of Bedford, and presumably other places, asking that children under 16 should be banned from cinemas on Sundays unless accompanied by an adult. The fact that specially selected films were shown only aggravated the matter in his eyes. Children went too frequently each week without having an extra reason to go on Sunday. He alleged that children crowded out war workers, servicemen and women, and others who had been the original reason for opening on that day. The Borough Council supported the Dean and wrote to the County Council asking for the age limit to be introduced.

At the end of 1944 many local churches argued that the need for Sunday opening of cinemas had ceased. The cinema managers said that if films were shown that were suitable for Sunday showing no problems should arise. The Borough Council agreed to test public feeling again in a poll. The result was that two-thirds of those voting wanted the cinemas open. The Council recommended that children under 14 years of age could only be admitted when accompanied by an adult.

Getting a film to the cinema

The cinema has had two further problems. The first concerns the booking of films. In the early days each cinema booked its own films from the distributors but as cinema circuits grew the tendency was to book films from the head office. Union Cinemas Limited who owned the 'Alma' cinema in Luton booked theirs in London while the Touring Talkie Picture Company who owned the 'Cosy' in Arlesey booked their films in Kings Lynn, Norfolk. Other cinemas still booked their films directly from the film company representatives. When the film was booked instructions had to be given how the film was to get to the cinema. Many had their films delivered to the nearest railway station such as Harlington LMS Station where the 'Picturedrome' in

Toddington went to collect theirs. Others had to use the bus company or special transport.

The early audiences

The first public performance of pictures in London is thought to have been that of the Cinematograph Lumière on 20 February 1896 at the Regent Street Polytechnic. The first London cinema is thought to have been in Balham in 1907. Big business had appeared in the shape of Provincial Cinematograph Theatres Limited by 1909. By 1914 at least 3,500 cinemas were in existence.

Edwardian audiences were youthful and predominantly working class. The middle class were condescending as they were to be towards television. Many who went to the cinema were not former patrons of theatres or music halls so were a new public. Courting couples could watch the picture and share each other's company in semi-darkness.

The attraction of the cinema

The cinema became the entertainment of the masses during the First World War. They needed relaxation from the rigours of wartime and desired to know what their sons and husbands were experiencing at the front. The newsreel picture would give them some idea of that. The cost of a good evenings entertainment would only be a few pence so was relatively cheap. It provided an alternative to the public house and had had the added attraction that all the family could go out together. It must be remembered that the cinema preceded radio and television by many years. Going to the cinema often involved waiting in a queue to get in. This was a time for conversation among the family and with friends standing nearby. Patrons were admitted during the continuous performance of films. Once inside the usherette guided you to your seat with a torch, pointing out the vacant seats by shining her beam on them. People sitting in the same row would have to stand up to allow the newcomer to pass, inwardly groaning because they missed part of the film. During the interval between films the ice-cream girl would stand in a spot-light at a strategic point with her tray selling a variety of ice-cream, drinks and sweets. In the very early days cigars and cigarettes were sold. Many cinemas also entertained the public with unit organ music which had replaced the orchestra when movies became talkies. Just before the next feature film was shown a short film extract, known as the 'trailer', designed to

whet appetites for the next week's programme would be screened. This would be followed by local advertisements. Should an urgent message be received by the manager for a patron it could be superimposed upon the screen. Health-conscious managers would spray the cinema with 'Pinozone spray air purifier' which the makers claimed would destroy all microbes and germs so preventing disease. They aimed to make the badly-ventilated building sweet-smelling and pure.

Decline – wide screen, 3D, etc.

As the number of patrons fell after the Second World War, midnight matinées were introduced in order to attract patrons in after other forms of entertainment closed, and were successful for a time in some places. A special film was often shown. Other ideas were more successful, such as Cinerama and Vistavision. Children's clubs were very popular on Saturday mornings in many places.

As the number of racial minorities grew special films were shown for them with the actors and actresses speaking Hindi, Italian or Polish. These special shows were often shown Saturday or Sunday mornings – and still are.

Despite all these efforts to attract patrons many cinemas had to close; especially after the nationwide coverage by television. Many of the larger cinemas were converted into groups of smaller ones in order to show contrasting programmes in the same building, so increasing their potential audience. However, there are signs now of a movement back to the cinema with the public wanting some of the closed cinemas reopened.

Part two
The individual cinemas

Ampthill

Picturedrome Arthur Street (formerly Ossory Place). The old Salvation Army Barracks which had been built about 1890 were adapted in 1910 into the Picturedrome. Seating 200 people it showed silent films that were projected by a hand-operated projector. The film was accompanied by Newbury Stanbury on the piano. The cinema aimed to show the latest and most up-to-date animated pictures with a programme changing twice a week, and with additional performances on Tuesdays and Saturdays. People from neighbouring villages came in on Saturdays to have a good time, and to sing or jeer when the film broke. They paid 1s, 6d and 3d to get in.

Open only a few years the building is now two houses, and the projection box is still identifiable on the outside of one.

The Electric Kinema in Saunders Piece was opened about 1923 by Mrs Alice Price, who sold it to the Southan Morris Circuit by 1928. It later changed its name to the **Kinema**. The building was erected in 1870 as a Primitive Methodist Chapel. As a cinema it had an electrically operated projector worked by Ernie Webb of Maulden, assisted by Ken Googe. Entrance money of 6d to 1s 3d was taken by Mrs Edna Beck. The screen was set up high on the wall. The lighting was by electricity with chinese lanterns hung from the ceiling. Oriental-style pictures hung on the walls.

In the early days the programme usually included a *Felix the cat* cartoon. Tom Mix and his horse were also popular favourites. Before the introduction of the proper talkie films MGM produced *Ben Hur* starring Ramon Navaro and Francis X. Bushman in 1927, and this was shown in Ampthill with added sound-effects.

A later manager was Mr Bernard who is remembered as wearing steel-rimmed spectacles and a waxed moustache. He was a lively pianist and accompanied the films himself. When completely full, additional chairs were borrowed from houses in the street to cope with the overflow. A special matinée on Mondays was arranged for night-shift workers at the local brickworks.

The manager in 1936 was J. F. Mongiardino, who stood for the town council but came bottom of the poll.

The builing closed as a cinema before the outbreak of the Second World War before being requisitioned by the military in 1940. The County Council converted it to a Branch Library in 1949, in which capacity it is still doing valiant service.

1   The Picturedrome, Ampthill.

III The Zonita, Ampthill.

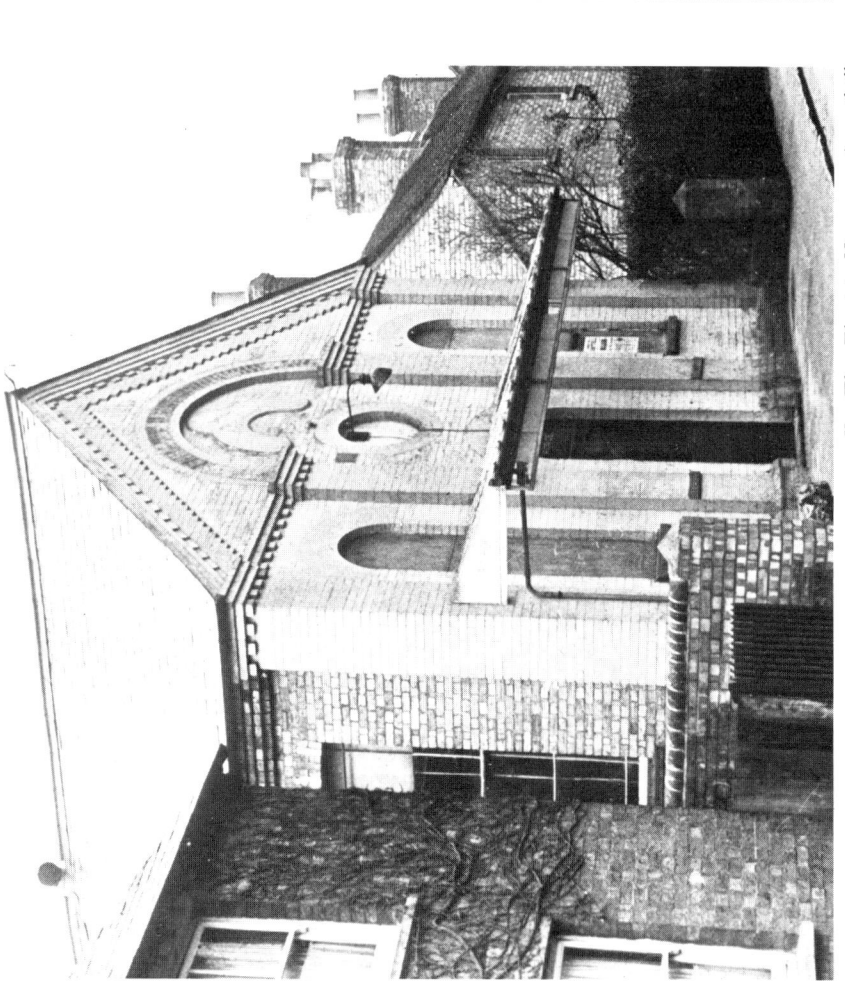

II The Electric Kinema, Ampthill.

Zonita, Bedford Street. The plans for this building on what was part of an old brewery site were approved by the Stage Plays Performance Committee of the County Council on 29 May 1937, and by the Urban District Council soon after. It had a circle, so was luxurious when compared with the Kinema which soon closed. Fred Valder was the popular manager for many years.

During the war period there was a rush after the last film to catch the bus home. As it was the largest hall in Ampthill the service to mark the end of the war was held in the Zonita in 1945. The service being led by the Chairman of the Urban District Council.

Later that year 400 local children went to see films as part of the peace celebrations. On a more controversial note the owners had a proposal to open on Sundays taken to a public meeting and then to a referendum. In the latter 591 people supported the open on Sunday appeal, while 562 opposed it. The Stage Plays Committee approved opening at 6.15 pm on Sunday in 1948.

The cinema finally closed in 1960 due to increasing overheads. The Cox Cinema Company had sold it to R. Chetham of Bedford in 1952. The building is now part of the Roses Fashion Centre Organisation.

Arlesey

The **Cosy Cinema**, Hospital Road, was first licensed in 1920 as the **Victory** by Mr S. C. Gray of Sandy; provided that the County Surveyor approved the building, and also on condition that no re-winding of films took place during the time the building was being used for 'exhibitions'.

An early manager was William Sinclair Cotter who had his daughter as projectionist. Cotter was a professional actor who put on stage shows in aid of charity. On Saturday nights he would move the seats and hold dances. He is remembered as charging half price to the unemployed in the 1920s. Mr F. W. Kirby took over as proprietor and manager in the late 1920s running the cinema with only one projector so you had to wait for a reel to be changed.

The cinema closed for a time until a Mr Jackson took over. He used to run a raffle on Friday nights and one man remembers his father winning a joint of meat. Unfortunately the cinema had to close again to be reopened as the **Premier** in the 1930s by Mr A.H. Street, 4 The Gardens, Arlesey Road, Stotfold. **Mr Street** had 2 film projectors using Morrison Sound Equipment and a slide projector. During this period the film *All Quiet on the Western Front* was shown. Three Counties Bus Companies were entrusted with carrying the new films to Arlesey. The cinema now opened nightly and three times on Saturday but still did not pay so it had to close again.

About 1935 the cinema was taken over by the Touring Talking Picture Company of King's Lynn, Norfolk. They redecorated the cinema, put in a sloping floor and curtained the stage which was illuminated by coloured lights. The projection room was re-modelled for the Gyrotone Sound equipment to show once nightly and twice on Saturdays when seats cost 6d to 1s 3d. The company booked the films in King's Lynn and arranged for road transport to get them to Arlesey. Their first manager was Mr B. Plum from Heacham, Norfolk to be succeeded by Frank Bryant, Frank Saunders and finally by Mrs E. Dalton of Arlesey. The Cosy Cinema Company of Buntingford, Hertfordshire later bought the cinema and ran it until it had to close again about 1958.

The iron-built building was owned by Charles Wells Brewery and shook when trains passed nearby. 160 patrons could be seated at one time. By 1949 neighbouring households were complaining of noisy machinery housed in an extension built on to a brick wall that was only three feet away from their houses, the noise preventing their children sleeping. Safety always seems to have been a problem to the authorities with

IV *The Cosy, Arlesey.*

defective seating and worn carpeting inside, and piles of coke blocking exits from the outside.

Mr E. G. Randall of Potton tried to reopen the cinema by running limited performances for children but it finally closed in June 1962. The building is now used as a store by a local builder who still rents it from the brewery.

Bedford

The townsfolk of Bedford were introduced to the cinema by the Blake brothers, Ernest and William, who as early as 1897 were showing the 'animatograph'. By 1909 they were establishing the first cinema at the **Association Hall** on the corner of Silver Street and Harpur Street which belonged to the YMCA (now Braggins). The Grand Opening programme of Monday, 3 May 1909 showed the Cup Final at Crystal Palace, and a series of short films – *The Stowaway* in which a boy stows away and on his return finds that his drunken mother has reformed, *Uncle's Picnic* where two naughty boys cause trouble, *The Kitchen Maid's Dream* a romance, and the *Money Lender's Mistake* in that he abducts a girl in his car and is pursued by her lover on a cycle. No actors and actresses were given star billing so the film attracted on the title alone in those days. The programme was changed weekly and was shown twice nightly at 7 and 9 pm with prices at 2d, 3d, 4d and 6d. Blakes were at the Association Hall only a short time as they opened the 'Picturedrome' in 1910. In 1903 Ernest was to join Kodak at 45s a week and rose through the ranks to become Chairman in 1946 at £20,000 a year.

The other cinema owners in Bedford were Robert and William Chetham who were cousins. They had a boatbuilding business at Batts Ford and at the town bridge. The Picturedrome was built on their land and was leased by the Blake's who ran it until the Chethams took over after the First World War. The cousins soon divided their interests with William taking the boatbuilding business and Robert the cinemas. Mrs Robert Chetham booked the films and did the office work. At this period the cinema had to pay the film company 45 per cent of the takings, for which they got in return the main feature and sometimes a second film.

The Empire, 27 Midland Road was opened by Blake Brothers (Theatres) Limited in 1915 and closed by Granada (Bedford) Limited on 20 June 1977. The cinema could seat 160 patrons in the circle and 374 in the stalls. By 1917 there were two complete 'exhibitions' each day beginning at 7 and 9 pm, with matinées on Wednesday and Saturday at 3 pm. The Empire opened specially for 'elementary school children' on Fridays at 4.30 pm. The venture prospered and by 1925 there were three programmes a day with two new programmes each week, and ten years later the cinema was open continuously from 2 pm to 11 pm. Talking pictures arrived in 1930, and Cinemascope in December 1954 when there was a grand opening by the Mayor, the ceremony being filmed by the Crest Film Group. The Empire was the second cinema in Bedford

HAROLD LLOYD

in

College Days

THE MADDEST, MERRIEST, COMEDY THE SCREEN HAS EVER SEEN.

All Bedford will ring with the roars of laughter at Harold in the Football Match.

ALL NEXT WEEK
At 3, 7 & 9.

Exclusive to

THE EMPIRE

Bedfordshire Times. January 1926.

V   Association Hall, Bedford.

to get Cinemascope. Granada (Bedford) Limited had bought the Empire in the mid-1930s. The early sound equipment had been Western Electric Sound, but by 1960 'Projectomatic 'O'' equipment was in use with Zenon lanterns and rectifiers. R. Ernest Blake who had been the manager for many years retired on the 15 January 1966. His successor attempted to revive trade in 1970–71 by introducing midnight matinées. This move was successful for a period but the Empire closed at short notice in the Autumn of 1975 for some weeks as it was said that there was a 'shortage of worthwhile films'. It had been showing a mixture of sex, horror and reissued films for some time. It reopened in April 1976 after being overhauled and became known as

Granada 3, with only one performance each day. There were soon new threats to close the cinema despite the Bedford Society deploring the possible loss of the 65-year-old building. Demolition took place in the autumn of 1977 together with a café on the adjoining site.

The Empire was the cinema at which the Stage Plays Committee of the County Council viewed the more controversial films.

Eastern Electricity now have a showroom on the site.

VI   The Empire, Bedford.

The Granada, St Peter's Street. The Granada was opened by Lord Ampthill, the then Chairman of Bedfordshire County Council, at 8 pm Saturday, 15 December 1934. He spoke of it being a contribution to the well-being of the people of Bedford and also of the County. The Chairman of Granada (Bedford) Limited at the time, Sir Thomas Keens, who was a Luton man, also spoke.

The programme which was issued at the time gave some details of the building of the cinema which took 5½ months. Of the 233 men directly employed 190 were from Bedford and the immediate district. Men and women from 49 other firms throughout the world were also involved. The programme told how electric wire comes from Southampton, silk damask from Bradford, bricks were from Peterborough, Wilton carpet came from Heckmondwicke and 1,250 square yards of linoleum was bought from Kirkcaldy. Firms in Malaya, Trinidad, Italy and Spain supplied rubber, asphalt, marble and cork while parts of the Wurlitzer organ were made in North Tonawanda, USA. Floodlighting equipment was erected on St Peter's Green in 1935.

The first film shown was *The Thin Man* starring William Powell and Myrna Loy, with Laurel and Hardy in *The Private Life of Oliver the Eighth*. It cost 9d and 1s 3d for a seat in the stalls, 1s 6d in the circle, 2s and 2s 6d in the loges, and finally if you went by car it cost 6d to park it. During the interval of the first performance Harold Betts played the £3,000 Wurlitzer organ.

Stage performances became a feature in the 1930s, and on one occasion 'Les Apache Accordian Band' played; with the second part of the programme being Cecil B. De Mille's *The Crusades* starring Loretta Young, Henry Wilcoxon and C. Aubrey Smith. The following week Reginald Dixon was booked to play the organ. The sound equipment at this period was RCA Photophone Limited.

The Granada became the first cinema in Bedford to have Cinemascope with a screen measuring 52 feet by 25 feet, the sound came from 14 speakers. The first film was *The Robe* featuring Richard Burton, Jean Simmons and Victor Mature. Jack Billing the acting manager said 'It could not be better'. There were long queues to see the new-style films. Later an even larger screen was introduced to cater for 70 mm film causing seats to be removed and part of the proscenium arch to be covered.

In the 1940s and 1950s childrens' matinées were very popular. A music system was installed in the foyer in 1954 as an added attraction using a 3-speed autochange system, which in turn was replaced by a tape system in 1958.

The café in the cinema had been run by the Bedford firm of Dudeney and Johnson for many years, but they gave up the lease in 1956. A beer, wine and spirit licence was taken out by the manager of Granada. When the café finally closed a second and smaller cinema took its place, being known as Granada 2 following the national trend of showing contrasting films in one building. In 1978 there was a proposal to re-introduce the sale of alchohol.

The Palace, 58–60 High Street. In May 1911 plan number 5436 was deposited with the Borough of Bedford by Messrs Felce and Warner for the erection of a cinematograph theatre on the site of *Chequers Inn*. The full council went into committee to consider the plan be formally approved with the following rider 'that the attention of Bedfordshire County Council be directed to the point whether in the interests of and for the safety of the public an emergency exit should not be provided on the south side of the building'. The *Chequers* public house was largely undisturbed when finally adapted. The original owners were Bedford Palace Limited but they sold out to Granada in the 1930s.

In 1925, when the 'ebullient' Bill Kettle was the manager, the Palace was open daily from 3–5 pm and from 6.30 to 10.30 pm, Patrick Kettle, the son of the manager

They agreed to build a public convenience for both sexes and give it free of charge to the Borough. They also agreed to demolish the existing convenience and to fill it in before paving the area. 'Prices' also paid for moving a traffic signal controller. The deal further benefited the Borough in that they were given 11 feet of frontage for road improvements.

The Picturedrome, Duck Mill Walk. The Corporation of Bedford council minutes for December 1909 record that a plan for an electric theatre was deposited for Messrs Chetham, Sons and Biffen. The plan was approved by the Streets and Buildings Committee subject to satisfactory lavatory accommodation being installed. The plan

VII   The Palace, Bedford.

sang with the orchestra consisting of Donald Fraser on drums and Dorothy Edwards on piano, while in the foyer Ada Noble issued the tickets. In 1935 Wells and Winch had the licence to sell alcohol in the bar while John Mills and Lilli Palmer starred in *The First Offence*. The bar became John Collier's tailors shop. The last film shown was *Boys Will Be Boys* starring Will Hay and Gordon Harker, a film that had been adapted from Beachcomber's Narkover stories.

When the Palace was pulled down in 1936 Prices Tailors Limited the parent company of Colliers bought the site and proposed to build a block of shops on it

VIII   The Picturedrome, Bedford.

Dismantled Oct 1983　　　IX　　The Plaza, Bedford.

The Plaza, The Embankment. On Thursday 21 December 1911 there was a grand opening of the building for roller skating. Three sessions were held each day with a band for the afternoon and evening sessions. Roller skating went on for only a few years, before other events took over. Melba sang here, and both Lord Roberts and Lloyd George spoke. Trade fairs were also held from time to time. As the hall was so vast it had to be cut into two parts and the eastern end became a garage. The remaining part became the Café Dansant where dancing took place in the winter months and concert parties came for short seasons in the summer. When the public started to prefer going to the Corn Exchange for dances Robert Chetham first introduced boxing and then films. The next move was to 'rake' the floor and to raise the ceiling to accommodate the large screen.

The opening ceremony for the Plaza was performed by the film director Herbert Wilcox on the 4 March 1929. Harold Lloyd starred in the first film *Speedy*. The Stage Plays Committee's insistance that the iron railings and a brick wall that had

showing the proposed seating accommodation and gangways was generally acceptable but one corner had to be changed as it presented a possible source of danger in case of fire. At this stage no guarantee of a Stage Plays licence would be granted. The full Council rejected the plan but allowed the Streets and Buildings Committee to look at the lavatory accommodation again. The plan was finally approved in January 1910 subject to a WC being attached to the building with an entrance from inside. It was to be free during performances. As the Corporation was also the Electricity Company they could negotiate electricity charges with the lessees Blake Brothers. The supply to the projection equipment had to be paid for separately at a cost of 2d per unit. The interior and exterior lighting was to be paid for separately.

This was the first full-time cinema in Bedford and was leased by the Blake Brothers after their success at the Association Hall. W. H. and R. Chetham took over after a time and ran it until it closed in 1964. In the very early days the seats were schoolroom chairs, which in time were replaced by red plush seats. Advertised as being 'by the old stone bridge' the Picturedrome was open 3 times a day in 1926 with complete shows at 3, 7 and 9 pm. After showing 'high class animated' pictures for many years the cinema was the first to show talkies in December 1929. Formerly the public had been thrilled by the exploits of Zigomar, Nick Carter and Fantomas, and also enjoyed the added attraction of the Vivaphone which supplied the sound effects to support the orchestra's efforts. The latter was a cello, violin and baby grand piano. Now the new Western Electric Sound system took over. As the maintenance engineer for Western Electric lived in Bedford the management were able to confidently announce when the machine broke down that 'Western Electric have it in hand'. At this period a printed monthly programme was published to give patrons brief biographical details of the 'stars'. It was at the Picturedrome that the Bedford Film Society met in the late 1940s and early 1950s.

The film *Children of Hiroshima* was shown at this cinema in November 1955. this depicted the horrors following the dropping of the first atomic bomb, and had English subtitles. In an attempt to improve facilities for patrons 'Hurseal' oil-filled radiators were installed in 1957. This was important as there was always trouble with the floor rotting as sometimes the river flooded into the cinema in winter.

Cinemascope was introduced in July 1956, but this did not save the cinema as it was closed in 1964 with the last film being an X certificate one *A House of Sand*. The closure was not commented on by the local papers.

surrounded the Café Dansant be removed to allow a queue to form that did not obstruct passing traffic proved a wise move. With a proscenium width of 40 feet and seating for over 1,000 patrons it was a very versatile building. For a front seat costing 10d you could have watched Greta Garbo and John Barrymore in *Grand Hotel* in the 1930s.

Of the two cinemas owned by the Chetham family in Bedford the bigger films tended to be shown here. After being bought by the Granada chain it was renamed the 'Century', and they introduced children's matinées. It finally closed in June 1974. The Borough Council then wanted to demolish the building and to plant gardens, but after many objections it became the 'Nite-Spot' nightclub in 1975, and closed in 1980.

Proposed new picture theatres

There were two of these in Bedford. The first was to have been in Mill Street. We first learn of this when a letter of protest was sent to the Borough Council in April 1920 from the Bunyan Meeting. This caused the Council to prohibit the building of the cinema until it could be further considered. In July further representations were made by interested parties but an order delaying the building for a further three months was made because the provision of urgently needed dwelling accommodation was likely to be effected by labour shortages. In January 1921 the Public Works Committee asked the Housing Committee to consider the matter. They again heard the opinions of the builder and Bunyan Meeting, yet failed to take a decision, asking the Council to

decide. Later the 'Old Castle' Picture House (Bedford) Limited appealed to the Ministry of Health against an order made in February 1921 prohibiting building. A tribunal was arranged for 20 April 1921, but this was adjourned because of the National Emergency. The following month it was adjourned indefinitely.

When Granada (Bedford) Limited were wanting to build a cinema in Bedford they first considered an island site in Dame Alice street, but eventually decided to build in St Peter's Street. The site in Dame Alice Street carried a notice advertising the cinema for some years. It was used as a temporary car park in the 1950s before a new telephone exchange was built on it.

MARY PICKFORD "LITTLE ANNIE ROONEY" DIRECTED BY WILLIAM BEAUDINE

Biggleswade

Like many other places Biggleswade was first introduced to the cinema by travelling shows which set up on the Market Square. One of these was owned by Mr Charles Thurston the fairground proprietor. On one visit in September 1911 he discovered that Mr Hull of Gamlingay had erected his 'Electric Castle' (a grand up-to-date touring picture palace), on the Dolphin Meadow where he held shows twice nightly at 7 and 9 pm. Hull's programme advertised in the *Biggleswade Chronicle* was *The Sheriff's Chum* (a splendid western drama); *Rolling, Rolling* (a screaming comic film); *Trailed by an Indian* (drama); *Resurrection of John* (comic); *The Chief's Daughter* (another western drama); and *Courtship Rivals*. To see the programme on the Friday and Saturday you paid 3d, 2d and 6d. The 'Electric Castle' was a wood and canvas theatre, it spurred on Charles Thurston to buy land from the brewery and then to build the Empire cinema.

Empire Cinema, Hitchin Street, just before the First World War. In the early days a mixture of stage shows and films was offered to the public. For the week starting Monday, 14 February 1916 the programme was the film *The Torrent* which was in two parts. This was said to be a thrilling up-to-date drama. The other main attraction was on the stage where 'Le blond Trio' performed their sensational and daring balancing act on the revolving and breakaway ladder. They were also known as the aerial wonders. The latest war films were also featured. Six months later 'Waldo and Etoile' presented their effective, clever and refined novelty act which opened with the human crocodile and artistic dancing; and concluded with the limit in comedy, bending, tumbling, etc. The pictures that week included a serial, Pathé news and 3 films in either 2 or 3 acts. The theatre was disinfected daily with Jeyes fluid.

Four years later in February 1920 the film version of Sir Henry Irvine's great stage play *The Bells* was shown. The supporting programme included episode 9 of *Hands Up*.

Professional pantomime came to Biggleswade in February 1921 when Jackson Hartley brought his panto *Cinderella*. There were 8 scenes to enjoy featuring riotous fun and laughter, some good comedians, dancing, the latest songs, etc. The show had been given at the Tivoli Theatre, Manchester and the cast included Maudie Goodman as Cinderella and George Arnett as Buttons. The prices that week were 8d, 1s 3d, 1s 10d and 2s 4d; while the children's matinées were 5d, 9d, 1s 3d and 1s

The Empire, Biggleswade.

10d. Seats could only be booked at Cunningham's Music Store in Hitchin Street, Biggleswade.

Charles Thurston sold the Empire to Mr Hill of Biggleswade after a few years, and the Hill family sold it to the Cox Cinema Company in 1936. The early silent films were accompanied by a pianist seated in the orchestra pit.

The Empire had open gas fires in the early years to warm its 426 patrons. It closed in January 1958 due to declining custom, when the Company thought it best to concentrate their efforts on the Regal. AWH sound equipment was used by 1940. The building is now Pye Connectors Limited.

George's Hall, 67 High Street. This was an early competitor of the Empire, but had a short life as a cinema. The hall is now used for a multitude of events each year.

In the *Biggleswade Chronicle* for 11 February 1916 the programme for the following week was given. It featured Harry Kardoc on the stage who proclaimed himself as the handcuff king and an expert jail breaker. He was an Australian who had a sensational self-release and shooting act in which he was assisted by Madame Kardoc. The films on Monday, Tuesday and Wednesday were *Stars Change Their Courses*, the Keystone Cops, dramas and other comedies. The latter part of the week featured the *Little Prospector*, the third episode of *Exploits of Elaine*, and *Vanishing Jewels* a 2-reel film. Patrons paid 3d, 6d and 9d. There was a children's matinée on Saturdays at 2.30 pm. The pianist at this time was Miss Dorothy Ellis.

Six months later Kitty Wade appeared on the stage with her refined choruses, speciality dances, which included Dutch top boot dancing, she wore picturesque dresses and her act was both versatile and novel. The films for the first three days were *Legend of the Poisoned Pool*, Mary Pickford in *So Near Yet So Far*, and the third episode of *Black Box*. The programme for the end of the week was *Shocking Stockings*, *Blind Fury* and a 2-reel film *The Exploits of Elaine*. The advertisement told patrons that cycles were stored free in a locked room, no war tax was paid on one penny tickets for children's matinées. Here too the cinema was disinfected daily with Jeyes fluid.

Houdini appeared at 'George's Theatre' in February 1920 with Elmo also on the bill. The advert stated that 'Pictures at George's are georgeous'. It seems to have closed as a cinema later that year.

In 1936 Victor Lion presented his London pantomime from 13 January for a week. The cast of 18 presented *Red Riding Hood*, a feast without vulgarity which was a 'refined panto for young and old where you can follow the story'. Seats cost 6d, 9d. 1s and 1s 6d in the evening. Matinées cost children 3d, 5d and 9d on Thursday and Saturday at 2.30 pm (adults paid evening prices and the free list was suspended).

The Regal Cinema, Station Road. This was built in 1936 by A. Hill and Sons on a site formerly used by Maythorns, the coach builders. It was formally opened by Admiral Sir Lionel Halsey, GCMG, in the presence of representatives of the film industry and local dignitories. The star of the first film shown *Where There's a Will – Will Hay*, also made a speech. Other features on the bill for the first two days were the Gaumont British News, Buster Keaton, a Walt Disney Cartoon and *The Wonder Ship* which was a trip on the Queen Mary from Southampton to New York. The end

XI *George's Hall, Biggleswade.*

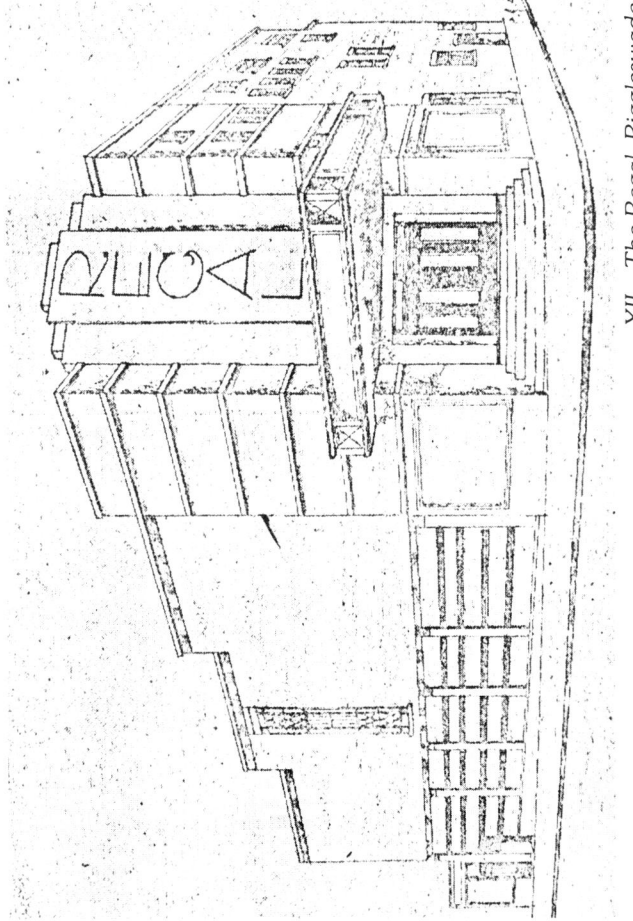

XII   *The Regal, Biggleswade.*

of the week had Tom Walls in *Pot Luck* another British film which also starred Ralph Lynn in the Michael Balcon picture. The second feature was *Coronado*.

In 1975 the Cox Cinema Company, who had bought it from the Hill's in 1937 sold out to the Regent Leisure Group who proposed closing the Regal to films. A petition with over 2,000 signatures persuaded them to close only part of the week, and to run bingo for the remaining time. Full time bingo began at Easter 1976. The last film shown at a matinée on the 30 April 1976 was *The Return of the Pink Panther.*

Cranfield

The Ritz was opened in July 1937 by the London and Provincial Cinemas Limited subject to alterations being made to improve safety aspects of the corridor leading to the projection room, and to proper ventilation of the re-winding room being provided. This was another cinema that had safety problems at intervals. As a result of reconstruction in 1949 standing room at the back was introduced for 24 people, and in the same year the Sunday opening hours were slightly changed to fit in with the

Sunday bus timetable. Cinemascope came to the Ritz in 1955. One manageress lived with her husband in two staff rooms that had no natural ventilation. There were complaints of cooking smells made to the County Council who asked Ampthill Urban District Council to investigate as a result of which the couple were given a council house. The cinema closed on 9 August 1960 because the Company could not afford to repair a leaking roof and to improve sanitary conditions. The Ritz had accommodation for 456 people, some of whom were seated on a raised balcony at the back.

The RAF requested that the Ritz be opened on Sundays in 1940 for the benefit of the servicemen stationed locally. The Rector objected most strongly each time the subject was raised, aided and abetted by local people. He seems to have lost on these occasions. A request to open Christmas Day 1940 was approved without much opposition.

Dunstable

The early history of the cinema in Dunstable is mainly one of attempts to build big developments which would include shops, assembly halls, and cinemas. One early pioneer called William Thompson employed a London architect (Max Zimmerman) to design such a complex at the corner of the High Street and Clifton Road. The plans were deposited with the Borough Council in June 1911 and showed an elaborately designed frontage to a building that held a cinema holding 517 people in the stalls and a further 171 in the gallery, four shops flanked the entrance which led through an outer and an inner hall to the cinema. There were dressing rooms and an orchestra pit below the stage. A ballroom was also included. The complex was not built, but William Thompson did have a short-lived cinema in the High Street about 1914.

Another cinema and shop complex was designed for the same site by F. Taperell and Haase of The Adelphi, London on behalf of their clients — Mill Street Development Syndicate Limited. This was very similar to the former plan and again was not built.

J. F. Marchant who had been giving performances whenever he could rent a film did manage to get his cinema designed and built on a site next to the Manor House garden. A Dunstable builder, George S. Wood, erected it for him. The Borough Council insisted that a fireproof operators' box was installed, and they also insisted that the whole building could be pulled down on 6 month's notice being given. There was no lavatory accommodation on the plan. The County Record Office has a sale bill advertising the cinema's auction on the 29 July 1914. It was advertised as a 'Picturedrome with stage, 2 dressing rooms, operating box reached by an iron staircase. It has a manager's office and one other room. The theatre is lighted by electric light.' The Borough of Dunstable seems to have had a mortgage on the

XIII   The Palace, Dunstable.

property. Included in the sale was an adjoining stone-built house with bay-fronted windows and 12 rooms. The sale of the whole being conducted at the Old Sugar Loaf Hotel, Dunstable.

Mr Marchant, a restauranteur, does not seem to have been put off because he

XIV   The Union, Dunstable.

deposited plans for another cinema in June 1919 for an adjacent site next to the post office. This was to become the **Palace Cinema** which was built between the old cinema and the Manor House, which was next to the post office proposed site. The architects were Franklin and Deacon of Luton. Measuring 35 feet by 98 feet the cinema held 400 in the stalls and 112 in the gallery. The programme of films shown was to change three times weekly with no breaks in the performances to clear the hall of patrons. He claimed to show the world's best pictures in the most up-to-date cinema.

The walls were originally painted French grey with white mouldings and a brown dado. Windows were provided to let in fresh air and sunlight to avoid musty smells. A low pressure hot-water system was used to heat the cinema. Two stairways led up to the balcony. The whole cinema was lighted by electricity. As a fire precaution the floors were concrete. The projectors were provided by Gaumont.

A matinée was held on Saturdays. The Palace was bought by the Southan Morris Circuit about 1930 and they introduced RCA Photophone Limited sound. The cinema finally closed in the late 1930s. It had been opened by the Mayor of Dunstable (Alderman W. E. Seamons) in front of a packed house. He said that the event was the highlight of his year of office. The first programme included the Pathé Gazette news, a Fox comedy and other features. The main film was *John Forrest Finds Himself.*

A contemporary cinema of the first Marchant cinema was planned for Charles Abrahams by A. Wilkinson of Victoria Street, Luton on the High Street North corner with Houghton Lane in 1913. This was to hold 264 people in a long narrow building that was to have a raked floor. Abrahams does not seem to have proceeded with the plan.

The **Union Cinema** was built on the site of the first Marchant cinema and next to his second. The cinema opened in 1937 and held 1,048 patrons in the stalls and a further 384 in the circle. A café was included in the plans drawn up by Leslie H. Kemp and Taskes of Great St James Street, London. The car park served both cinemas. The first owners were Union Cinemas Limited who were taken over by Associated British Cinemas in 1937. The cinema was a typical design for the 1930s and provided for Western Electric sound equipment to be used, and in order to widen the possible use of the theatre, an orchestra pit was included. By 1952 patrons' cars were blocking the side road to the car park, this caused difficulties for the people leaving the side exit from the stalls, so the manager was told by the Stage Plays Performance Committee to control the parking.

The first film shown in the Union after re-naming as the **ABC** was *A Summer Place*, with *A Question of Hospitality* as the second feature. It was at the Union that 2,500 children saw the Queen's Coronation film in 1953. Cinemascope was introduced in 1955, while bingo was tried in January 1969 on 3 days a week which increased to 2 sessions every weekday and one on Sundays by 1973. The premises were eventually adapted for bingo and as a result of which films could not be shown and the licence was refused by the Stage Plays Performance Committee. A subsidiary company of ABC now runs the bingo hall – Star Cinemas (London) Limited.

For several Christmases a tree was placed in the foyer to attract toys for sick children. In the early 1960s the Pakistani Film Society held their meetings at the cinema before going to the Ritz at Luton in 1963. In an attempt to attract custom, amusement machines and midnight matinées were tried in the late 1960s, as were special family shows, but the cinema finally closed in February 1973. The last film shown was probably *Fuzz* starring Raquel Welch (an X film) which was shown for 4 days starting 4 February.

There is now no cinema in Dunstable, although in 1971 a new cinema to be called The Galaxy, was proposed, but was not built.

Henlow

The Camp There was a cinema at Henlow Camp from the very early 1930s until after the Second World War for the benefit of the RAF who allowed local people to use it. The cinema was staffed by the RAF who showed training films during the day. Situated between the guardroom and the railway line to Hitchin the cinema held two performances each evening, and the programme was changed twice a week in order to show all the popular films of the day. In 1947 the RAF wrote to the County Stage Plays Performance Committee asking for permission to allow children to use the modest-sized cinema of 595 seats priced at either 6d or 1s. The sound equipment used was 'AWH Sound' and the Entertainments Officer booked the films through the Eastern Counties Film Service.

There was a change of name in the 1950s to the **Astra** and later it was closed to the general public.

Kempston

Plans for a cinema called the **Astoria** were submitted to the Urban District Council for Kempston in June 1934. This was to be in Bedford Road between the Methodist Chapel and Halsey Road. The architect was Jas. E. Adamson who was also employed by the Ashford Trust Limited. A Kempston company (Samuel Foster Limited) were the proposed builders. The cinema was to include seating for 570 people on the ground floor, an orchestra pit, two dressing rooms, a manager's office and a pay desk in the foyer, a balcony to seat 254 with accommodation next to it for a tea room and kitchen. There was also to be a projection room with its separate re-wind room, a workshop and a store. The total seating was to have been 824 seats. However, it was not built.

A further proposal for an 800 seat cinema was made by the Cox Cinema Company in 1937, but this was not built either.

Leighton Buzzard/Linslade

The Exchange, Corn Exchange, Lake Street. The building was erected in 1862 by a company formed from local businessmen who bought 450 shares in it at £10 each. The Corn Exchange eventually cost £7,000 to build. It was used for a wide range of public meetings and events, and had a purpose-built theatre in the rear. It had two large halls, the upper one being used as a Police Court in later years.

It was used as an occasional cinema in the 1920s but never became an established cinema. Special event films were shown such as Rudolph Valentino in *Four Horsemen of the Apocalypse* and D. W. Griffith's *Birth of a Nation*. The Exchange had a level floor and the patrons sat mainly on forms but some chairs were provided at the back. It was run by the Webb family who also managed the 'Old Vic'. They went on to run cinemas in Hemel Hempstead and Harpenden.

Douglas Fairbanks Snr. starred in the silent spectacular *Robin Hood*. Talkies were never shown here, and competition with the 'Oriel' closed it. Both cinemas being owned by Shipman and King.

The building fell into disuse in the 1950s and was demolished in 1966.

The Grand Leighton Road, Linslade. This was another multi-purpose building that was erected with 4½ inch walls by Thomas Yirrel's the builders of Bridge Street, Leighton Buzzard. It was opened in 1922, when it was known as the **Empire** for a few months. The Grand was the area's first purpose-built cinema. Local people took to it quickly, liking the banked seating with comfortable leg room. It was typical of that generation of cinemas and held 500 people in balcony and stalls.

The first manager was a Mr G. H. Blackburn and the music was provided by Rosie Rowe on the piano with Richard Anderson on the violin and musical saw. The projector was worked from electric batteries that needed recharging by a gas engine at intervals to improve the picture on the screen.

On 21 February 1922 a special announcement said that the film for the second part of the week was *Mrs Erricker's Reputation*. The announcement is interesting in that it included a long appreciation of the film by the author, Thomas Cobb, who said that the film was produced by Cecil Hepworth and the acting of Miss Alma Taylor in a difficult role was as 'charming as her appearance'. The advertisements in following weeks continued the practice of including an appreciation.

Special afternoon shows were given for 'the benefit of country visitors' within weeks of opening. The continuous evening programme ran from 6 to 10.15 pm. The film of the Oxford and Cambridge boat race was shown for three days from 25 April 1922 when the film was based on Ethel M. Dell's book *Bars of Iron*. Another film made from an Ethel M. Dell book was shown on the 23 May 1922 and was called *The Prey of the Dragon*, and was produced by Stoll. The cinema then closed for the summer, and for alterations.

The name was changed to the **Grand** before it reopened on 1 August 1922, when Viola Dana starred in a spritely adaptation of the stage play *The Chorus Girl's Romance* which had been written originally by F. Scott Fitzgerald.

The August Bank Holiday matinée was *Madonnas and Men*, a film that we are

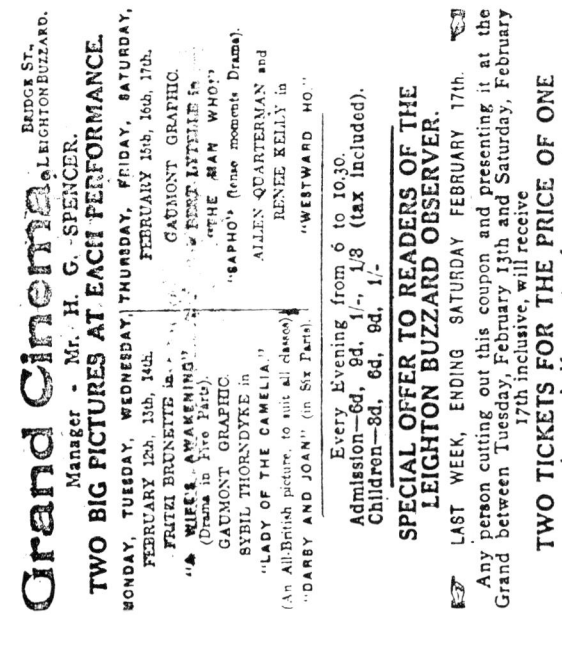

Grand Cinema, BRIDGE ST., LEIGHTON BUZZARD.

Manager - Mr. H. G. SPENCER.

TWO BIG PICTURES AT EACH PERFORMANCE.

MONDAY, TUESDAY, WEDNESDAY, THURSDAY, FRIDAY, SATURDAY,
FEBRUARY 12th, 13th, 14th.   FEBRUARY 15th, 16th, 17th.

FRITZI BRUNETTE in   GAUMONT GRAPHIC.
"A WIFE'S AWAKENING"   BERT LYTELL in
(Drama in Five Parts).   "THE MAN WHO"
GAUMONT GRAPHIC.   "SAPHO" (three moments Drama).
SYBIL THORNDYKE in   ALLEN QUARTERMAN and
"LADY OF THE CAMELIA."   RENEE KELLY in
(An All-British picture, to suit all classes)   "WESTWARD HO"
"DARBY AND JOAN" (in Six Parts).

Every Evening from 6 to 10.30.
Admission—6d, 9d, 1/-, 1/3 (tax included).
Children—3d, 6d, 9d, 1/-

SPECIAL OFFER TO READERS OF THE LEIGHTON BUZZARD OBSERVER.

☞ LAST WEEK, ENDING SATURDAY FEBRUARY 17th.

Any person cutting out this coupon and presenting it at the Grand between Tuesday, February 13th and Saturday, February 17th inclusive, will receive

TWO TICKETS FOR THE PRICE OF ONE
plus one halfpenny tax, for any seats.

Leighton Buzzard Observer. 13 February 1923.

XV The Exchange, Leighton Buzzard.

told posed three questions – are our moral standards lower than our forefathers, do you agree that a nation should be judged by the treatment of women, and do you know how long the sacrifice of women has amused the world?

Another special advertisement on 14 October 1922 said 'The management desire to point out that every effort has been made to make the theatre as comfortable as possible and visitors will find a great improvement, particularly in respect to warmth!

Sound films were first shown in Leighton Buzzard at the Grand. Notable films shown included *All Quiet on the Western Front* and Boris Karloff as *Frankenstein*. Shipman and King bought the original owners out who closed it soon after the 'Oriel' opened. The Grand never really paid as it was so small. The Building is now owned by SAH Limited who use it as a car showroom.

The Oriel Cinema. Lake Street. Situated opposite the Corn Exchange the Oriel was converted from the former home of a Dr Lawford by a consortium of local businessmen in December 1922. They had to agree to name the new cinema after the oriel windows in the original house, which had taken two years to adapt. The design was based on a West End theatre. It was heated at first by gas but later a hot air apparatus capable of pumping hot air at a temperature of 150°F was added.

Norma Talmadge starred in the opening film *Smiling Through*. Norma Talmadge was an American who owned her own production company. The supporting film was *Whose Wife?* with Billy West in the lead. A Pathé Gazette news was also shown.

The next film was *Tilly of Bloomsbury* starring Edna Best and Tom Reynolds. This was supported by *The Great Elephant Kraal* which depicted the dangers of elephant hunting.

The Oriel was sold to Shipman and King early in 1932. It was later sold to EMI Cinemas.

Silent films were originally shown by the local owners, but did not really pay until the building was leased to a larger company. The first talkie shown here was the *Gold Diggers*. Continuous performances were introduced from just before the war. The last film shown just before the Second World War was *The Little Princess*, starring Shirley Temple in her first technicolour romance, with the Jones family in *Everybody's Baby* as second feature. The Oriel was closed on the outbreak of war in September 1939, in common with all other cinemas. It reopened on Monday 11 September 1939, when the film starred Nelson Eddy in *Let Freedom Ring*, with

Humphrey Bogart in *Where Are Such Fools* as supporting feature. It was during the war that the cinema was most profitably aided by support from the airmen of RAF Stanbridge. Cine-concerts were a popular weekend feature. Civil Defence and Home Guard training films were shown to those organisations when the cinema was closed to the public.

One employee remembers the staff being inspected by the manager each day before the show began to see if they had clean shoes, well-pressed trousers and tidy hair.

The Oriel seated over 800 people of whom 326 were in the circle. The circle was not seated at first as it was thought unnecessary. The curtains were made of a heavy material and the carpets were a thick heavy-duty quality. These with the plush seating kept the background noise down, so necessary once talkies came in.

An early example of special permission being given to open on a Sunday was when the Rev Ernest Scott was allowed to show films to Boy Scouts on Sunday, 5 October 1924. However, the Scouts were refused permission in 1930 to show their Jubilee film. On Good Friday 1952 Cecil B. De Mille's *Samson and Delilah*, a top money-spinner, starring Hedy Lamar was shown together with a newsreel. On 17 July 1953, the Coronation film was shown to schoolchildren.

The cinema was converted to bingo in 1972, but in 1976 the board of EMI Cinemas and Leisure Ltd. investigated the viability of returning to films, as they were doing well in the country at that time – but so was bingo.

The Victoria Electric Palace. Hartwell Grove. Later called the Old Vic, this was a corrugated iron building with a steel span roof and brick walls. Originally built as a piano and organ store by the Purrett family in 1910, it was soon taken over by Captain F. Webb (a well-made six-footer) and his family; Larry was projectionist, Fredrica was in the box office and Sybil played the grand piano. They were there until about 1912 showing pictures two or three nights a week until business picked up, and then more frequently. The Victoria was giving two performances every night in the early 1920s. Rather old films were shown with a few epics featured. There were only a few hundred patrons. Charlie Chaplin and the Keystone Kops were very popular. Custom gradually drifted to the 'Grand' and its better facilities.

The Victoria was another cinema that needed to charge its batteries from a gas engine. A later projectionist was Sam Powell while the accompanist was a Belgian,

Luton Reporter, 1909.

Leighton Buzzard Observer, 1923.

Monsieur Piron, assisted by his English-born wife on the violin.

After closing in the 1930s a good dance floor was put in and it became a palais de danse, with occasional boxing, wrestling and wedding receptions being held there. The Victoria was demolished in 1960.

Luton

The early film shows in Luton were held in tents pitched in Wardown Park or in the Corn Exchange, Plait Hall, or the Town Hall. One organisation that saw the advantages of the new entertainment was the Salvation Army who sought to combat the evils of drink. A hall at the back of the *Red Lion Hotel* was also used at times to show pictures.

An itinerant picture company which gave shows in various halls in Luton was 'Jury's Imperial Animated Pictures'. They claimed that their films were the 'perfection of animated photography' and that the company was the 'King of the all' and that 'We lead, others follow who can'. Starting 19 April 1909, they held a short season at the Corn Exchange with shows once nightly at 8.15 pm, doors being open at 7.45 pm. There was a grand illuminated matinee on the Saturday at 3pm with special prices for children. The advertisement in the *Luton Reporter* stated that 'Mr Jury has great pleasure in presenting the great international football match *England v Scotland*. This had been played at the Crystal Palace on Saturday, 3 April when England gained the championship of 1909.' Later in the month he held contests for the most handsome man and most beautiful lady in Luton. Silver watches were given as prizes. A baby competition for babies under 12 months was also held. The acting manager was named as Mr Dudley Harcourt.

During the First World War there were six commercial cinemas in Luton: while during the Second World War eight were open.

The Alma At the corner of Alma Street and New Bedford Road. This was a purpose-built cinema which was opened at Christmas 1929, on a site that had previously held shops and houses. Plans were prepared for a local businessman, Sydney Charles Dillingham, by the leading cinema architect of the day, George Coles. The main contractors were Douglas Halse and Co Ltd, of Woolwich, SE18. The site lay at the corner of Alma Street and New Bedford Road, and was on several of the main tram routes in Luton and was also within easy walking distance of two main bus terminals. The sloping site meant that the main entrance had to be next to the stage and not at the back of the cinema, above were the ballroom and a café. The 1,664 seats were shared between the circle and the stalls. The auditorium was decorated in beige and gold, with gold carpets. The proscenium was 49 feet wide and the stage 25 feet 6 inches deep. There were seven dressing rooms. The projection room was equipped with three simplex projectors with Western Electric sound-on-film and sound-on-disc and Magnascope equipment, a slide lantern and two spotlights. The normal 27 feet screen was increased to a Magnascope width of 40 feet some 20 years before the 'introduction' of wide screen. The fully equipped building cost about £128,000.

The opening ceremony took place at 7.30 pm on Saturday 21 December 1929, and was performed by the Mayor, Alderman Murry Barford, JP, CC, and the local MP, Dr E. Leslie Burgin. There were no musicians in the theatre but a ladies orchestra played in the café. However, the opening show included the Luton Band and the first film was of the New York Philharmonic Orchestra playing Wagners *Overture to Taunhauser*. The main film was the First National Pathé synchronised feature *The Divine Lady*, starring Corinne Griffith, the climax of which was the Battle of Trafalgar and for this the Magnascope was used. The programme beginning 30 December including Maurice Chevalier in *Innocents of Paris* an early all talking sound-on-film picture.

About this time the Alma made the national news as the first cinema to stop an express train – the deep red lights in the globe were apparently in line with signals on the up fast line to the north of Luton LMSR Station and were mistaken for a distant stop signal, so the colour was changed to blue.

An organ was introduced in 1930 as were variety shows and an 18-piece orchestra under J. Haydn Fawcett. The two manual six-unit Compton organ was opened on Monday, 5 May 1930, by the firm's demonstrator Herbert A. Dowson, with Mr

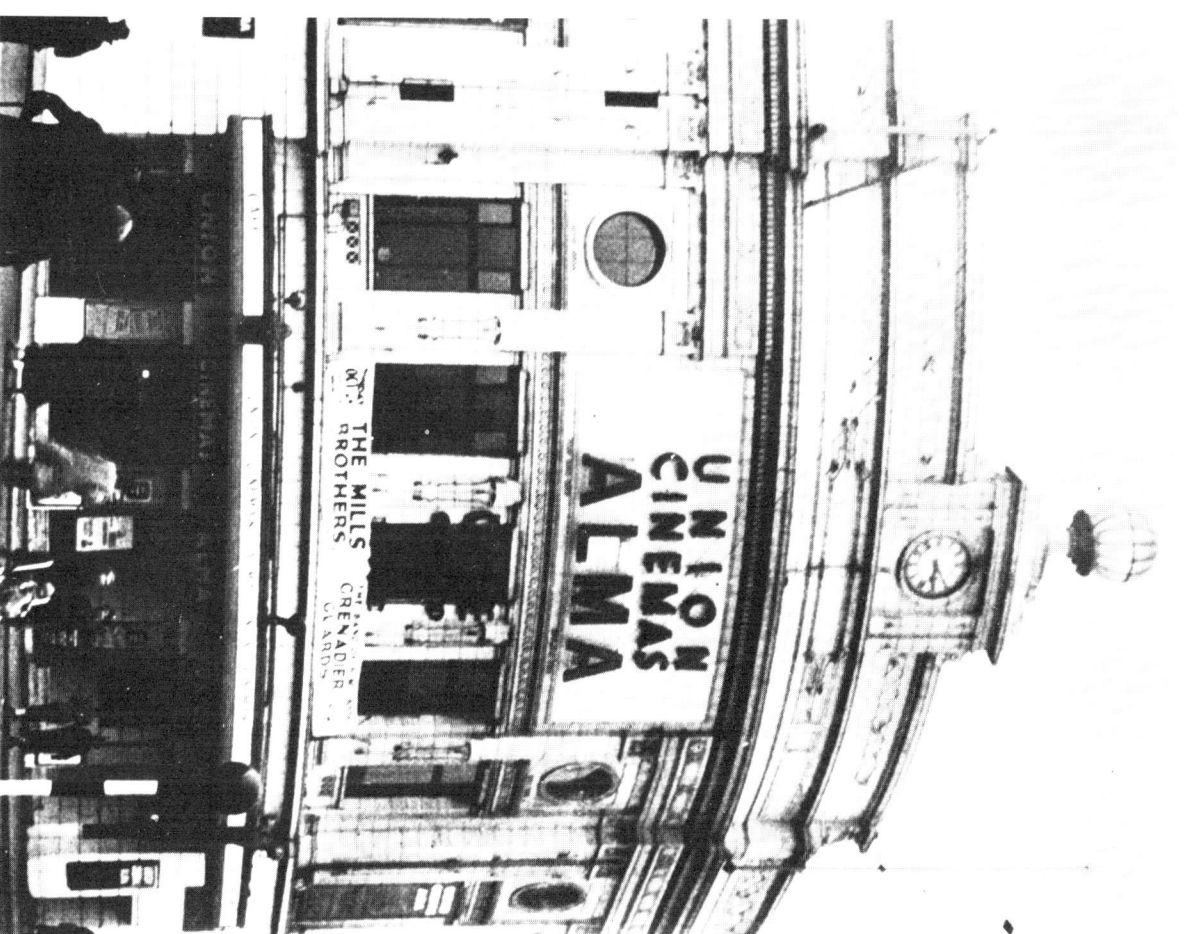

XVI *The Alma, Luton.*

Birmingham as the first resident organist. The orchestra always presented a programme on the stage with two grand pianos. J. Haydn Fawcett left in October 1930 to be followed by Sydney Phasey.

The Sunday opening of cinemas was not usual in the provinces at this time but Sunday concerts were permissible, provided no make-up was used. The first concert at the Alma was on 3 March 1935, and the acts included Troise and his Mandoliers, Beryl Orde (impressionist), Tessie O'Shea and Herschel Henlere. Later concerts featured Jack Hylton and his band and Harry Roy and his orchestra.

Combined tickets for lunch in the café and the show were introduced in 1936 (2s).

On Monday, 18 October 1943, the theatre went over to twice nightly variety, the first bill included Robb Wilton and the xylophonist Teddy Brown. The pit orchestra was conducted by the former cinema organist Harry Davidson who was to find fame on the radio with the old time dancing programme. *Those were the Days*. There were annual pantomimes for a large part of the 1940s and 1950s. There was a return to films on Monday, 17 January 1944, for a short time, interspersed with stage shows. The last film was *Utah* featuring Roy Rogers, and the programme also featured Errol Flynn in *Four's a Crowd*. The last stage show was *This was the army*. The theatre closed 17 July 1954. It was converted to the 'Cresta' Ballroom but was demolished in July 1960, to make way for a large shop and office block.

The cinema was owned in turn by a local businessman, Sydney Charles Dillingham; Leicester Square Estates Limited; Dillingham again; Reed's Theatres; Alliance Cinemas Limited, a subsidiary of Union cinemas. The last owner was ABC who leased it to a private company provided films were not shown and who converted it to the 'Cresta'.

The Empire, 116 Bury Park Road. When it opened on the 29 November 1921, the owners, Luton Cinemas Limited, claimed that there was no prospect of the cinema being superseded by anything better. The cinema served the Beech Hill and Leagrave Road districts and was very comfortable for the time. It was adapted from Mr E. L. Barber's aeroplane propellor factory by Seaward Brothers, Builders, and could seat 780 patrons on specially raised seats which were staggered on the balcony so that nobody would be directly in front of anyone else. The ceiling was packed with tin foil insulation. The foyer had panelled walls decorated with busts of a King and Queen, Charlie Chaplin, John Bull, Punch, and other busts representing comedy and

tragedy. The proscenium was decorated with Japanese designs and included concealed lighting behind tinted glass. The padded ledge of the balcony was the work of the trainees at the Government Instructional Factory at Chaul End. The first projection equipment to be used was two 'Simplex projectors' that were driven by motors made in Luton. By 1940. these had Western Electric sound equipment added.

The films at this period were accompanied by an orchestra comprising piano, violin and cello with Mr Reg Clarke as the musical director. The first film to be shown on 29 November 1921. was *Three Men in a Boat* made by Artistic Films Limited. During the interval Dorothy Longstaffe sang *Melisande in the Wood*. The film shown

XVII   The Empire, Luton.

in the second part of the week was *The White Dove*, starring the British actor H. B. Warner, who had gone to Hollywood about 1917. The management had a policy of showing one big feature film accompanied by a varied programme of shorts. They did not show serials, but in 1921 showed a series of films about football teams in training (Manchester United was the first). The first manager was W. Austin, who had 12 years experience in the industry working for film producers.

In 1926, the cinema was in trouble with the authorities for showing a film called *the Two Little Vagabonds* at a Saturday children's matinée despite a ruling that it was only suitable for adults. The film had been made in 1903 and told of how a gypsy whipped a boy for breaking a jug, and was whipped in turn by the local curate. How times change! The films were generally westerns but about 1928–9 the original film of *Ben Hur* was shown. Children's matinée prices were 2d, 4d and 6d to see a main film and serial. The cinema was sold to the Southan Morris Circuit by 1928, and was finally closed 15 October 1938.

The Grand Theatre, 25 Waller Street, staged mainly stage plays and variety shows, but between January to August, 1910, it was used as a cinema only. Out-of-the-ordinary films were shown at intervals afterwards. D. W. Griffith's film *Birth of a Nation* was given its public première there in 1914. The last film was probably the jungle epic *Simba* in April, 1930. The theatre was said to have a graceful circle and six prime boxes decorated with excellent gilt and white plasterwork. The Victorian building was one of two Bedfordshire theatres (the other was in Bedford), and was said to be the best in the East Midlands. It was opened at Christmas 1898, by Lily Langtry. The proprietor was W. Graham Falcon who was succeeded by his daughter Mrs R. Newton. Now pulled down it stood on part of the Arndale Centre site.

Anglo American Electric Picture Palace, 12 Gordon Street, first owned by the County Electric Pavilions Limited, later by Luton Electric Theatres Limited, when renamed Luton Electric Theatre. This was the first permanent cinema in Bedfordshire and could seat 400 people when it opened on 16 October 1909. The first show included 'Cinephone' shorts that were films synchronised to gramophone records.

The original policy of the cinema was to show short travel and comedy films to patrons paying 3d, 6d and 1s. On Saturday afternoons children could get in for 2d, 3d and 6d. The first advertisement placed in the *Luton Reporter* said that 'You may

Grand Theatre, Luton.

The above THEATRE is now Opened as a

Picture Palace

One House Nightly at 8.30.

SUBJECTS COMPRISING

Dramatic, Humorous,

Industrial, Hunting

and Travel,

TOGETHER WITH THE

Latest Pictures of Up-to-date

Events.

POPULAR PRICES :—

Gallery, 3d.; Pit, 6d.; Balcony and Stalls, 9d.; Circle, 1/-.

Children Half-Price to all parts except Gallery.

MATINEE, SATURDAY, at 3. Doors Open at 2.30.

XVIII   *The Anglo American Electric Picture Palace, Luton.*

EMPIRE

BURY PARK ROAD, LUTON

WEEK COMMENCING MONDAY JULY 12th.

MONDAY, TUESDAY & WEDNESDAY

CONWAY TEARLE and CLAIRE WINDSOR in

JUST A WOMAN

A tremendous Drama of Straying Husbands and Watchful Wives.

THURSDAY, FRIDAY & SATURDAY—

MILTON SILLS and DOROTHY MACKAILL in

THE MAKING OF O'MALLEY

A story of a hard hitting policeman who was hurt hit by Cupid.

come in at any time and see the performance right through. The very latest pictures are shown'. The programme beginning 25 October 1909 was *Hissian Renegades*, *The Vagabond's Adventure*, *The Message*, *Three Friends*, *The Seventh Buy*, *'He can't help it*, etc. They also offered singing pictures in addition—whatever they might have been. Another programme shown soon afterwards started at 6 pm and had a special picture for the week called *The Duke D'Enghein*, a beautiful coloured picture depicting a great tragedy from French history. It was supported by features on salmon fishing, Italian cavalry, China and *Race for a Monday*. The management claimed that there was no waiting at the doors. An early assistant manager became Mayor of Luton between 1947–49. (Councillor W. J. Edwards).

The *Luton News* reported in their edition for the 17 October 1929, that a fire took place on the 15 October. They included a picture showing the crowds watching the Fire Brigade putting it out soon after lunchtime. The Brigade had been notified at 7 minutes past 2 pm and did their job so well that one of the two engines attending was able to leave at 2.30 pm. Before they arrived Bernard P. Hyde of Gordon Street Garage entered the building with Police Constable Simpkins and tried to put out the fire with a chemical fire extinguisher. The curtains just inside the door were on fire and took all his efforts to put them out. During the fire the roof came off with what sounded like an explosion, and seats, walls and the screen were badly damaged. A lot of damage had been done in a short time. The second fire engine left at 3 pm. Two men were charged with arson.

The cinema was able to claim one achievement, that when the new public library in George Street was opened on the 1 October 1910, a film of the event was shown the same evening. Serials were first introduced in 1913. The first modern sound films were shown in early September 1929. The building was sold in April 1930 and a furniture shop took the site in August 1930.

The Library Theatre Central Library, St George's Square, was opened in November 1962. For the next seven years they were arranged by the Luton Film Society who had shown films at the old library since 1948. The first film in the new premises was *L'Aventura* on the 10 October 1962.

In 1969 the Society gave way to a Regional Film Theatre. The opening ceremony was attended by Sidney Reed, director of the British Film Institute at the time.

This cinema/theatre aims to provide a very wide range of attractions. Various professional companies appear at regular intervals presenting drama, ballet, opera, variety and children's theatre. Between September and April the Luton Music Club presents a series of concerts under the title of 'Music on Mondays' featuring top names in the world of music. The films shown are classic films and those for minority tastes. Special programmes for schools include plays, puppet shows, films and lectures. There are also shows put on by local amateur societies. There is seating for 257 patrons.

Odeon Cinema, 127 Dunstable Road. The Odeon is similar in plan to other cinemas built by that chain. It was opened on the 12 October 1938, to accommodate 2,000 patrons, the architect being London-based Andrew Mather. The ceremony was performed by the Mayor of Luton, Alderman J. T. Harrison, a feature of the ceremony was the band of the 1st Battalion King's Own Scottish Borderers. Champagne and caviare followed the ceremony. The building was air-conditioned and had BTH earphones for the partially deaf patron. With decoration inspired by the wife of the Managing Director of Odeon Cinemas (Mrs O. Deutsch) it aimed to be restful and yet modern. This care was necessary as the lights could be dimmed to show the film.

The first film was *The Drum*, starring Sabu, Raymond Massey and Valerie Hobson. During the war the BBC Symphony Orchestra, which had been evacuated to Bedford, often played at the Odeon in Luton.

As the County Council Stage Plays Committee was very careful about the kind of films shown on Good Friday, special permission had to be obtained in 1950 for *Three Little Girls in Blue* to be shown. While in the following December special performances during the school holidays also had to be approved. The following Easter programme included the film *Kim*.

Cinemascope was introduced in 1954, but unlike most cinemas there was no stereophonic sound. The cinema is still open but is converted into three cinemas.

The Palace Theatre, 19 Mill street, was later renamed the **Gaumont**, and then became the **Majestic Ballroom**. The firm that originally built the cinema is said to have gone bankrupt, but it opened 26 December 1912, with a mixed programme of variety, films and a ladies orchestra. It was apparently planned as a variety theatre with a gallery and circle. The circle staircase with a brass rail continued up to the spot box in the dome over the circle. Cine-variety continued up to the end of July 1932. The orchestra was that of Sydney Phasey. He was followed by Reg Fisher as leader when Phasey went to the Alma in 1930.

In 1929 the Stage Plays Committee had to consider a request from the manager to show *The King of Kings*, a film that had been refused a certificate by the British Board of Censors because they objected to the Saviour being depicted on the screen. Also in 1929 *The Singing Fool* starring Al Jolson attracted very long queues. In 1935 the technicolour film *Becky Sharp* was shown. The last films to be shown when the cinema closed in October 1961, were *Whisky Galore* and the *League of Gentlemen*. Ardente deaf aids were fitted. When a pit was dug for a Wurlitzer organ seepage from the River Lea caused abandonment of the scheme. Bingo is now run from the 17 feet deep stage.

The Picturedrome, 87 Park Street. This was the second cinema to open in Luton. It was owned by Luton Picture Limited, part of the Lion circuit. The advertisement in the *Luton News* of 6 April 1911, carried the special programme for the opening on 8 April. An interior and an exterior photograph were included as well as a statement that 'Every care has been taken to ensure the absolute comfort of patrons, and only the latest films obtainable will be shown'. Seats costing 9d on the 60-seated balcony could be booked in advance, while two-thirds of the stalls cost 3d and the rest 6d. All 500 seats were plush covered. High class music was provided by Mr R. A. Laidlaw's orchestra, of five players, while the staff of the resident manager (Mr Stephen Slinger) sold refreshments, cigars and cigarettes. The films shown included *In Perfect Harmony*, *Happy-Go-Lucky Jim* and *Tontolini Automobilist*, and seven other short films.

A regular advertisement at this period was, 'It's a fact, pictures being shown at

XIX   The Picturedrome, Luton.

Luton Picturedrome, Park Street, are simply beautiful'. Trams passed the door every four minutes.

For three days from 12 December 1921, the cinema showed Goldwyn's famous picture *The Old Nest*, a 10,000-foot long film, which would be on more than one

XX *The Savoy, Luton.*

reel. The story was based on the fact that 'There is no love like mother love and no home like the old nest'.

Owned by the Southan Morris Circuit by 1929 it was leased to Union Cinema Company by 1936 who closed it in October 1937.

The Picturedrome and High Town Electric Theatre, 24 High Town Road, opened on 24 August 1912, to show English, American and continental films. The proprietors said that the cinema would be 'No flash in the pan, but a high quality of programme will be maintained at all times. The cinema will be the only hall in Luton always showing the world famed Pathé Animated Gazette: an up-to-date topical budget, showing the world's events day by day. It is issued and received twice weekly on Wednesday and Saturday. Don't delay your visit.' special attention had been given to the arrangement of seating which was upholstered in plush covering throughout.

The programme changed on Mondays and Thursdays, with continuous performances between 6 and 11 pm, Saturdays between 5 and 11 pm, at a charge of 3d and 6d on the ground floor, and 9d and 1s in the Grand Circle, which could be reserved. There was a children's matinée every Saturday at 2 pm, with prices of 1d 2d and 3d. 'Picture play chocolates' were sold in the hall at reasonable prices, as were packets containing the photograph of a popular picture artist.

The first programme was a series of eight short films with only two of them being British – *The Chauffeur's Dream*, in which he dreamt of driving under the sea and down a volcano (made in 1908 and lasted 7 minutes), and *Amorous Arthur*, where a girl's sister replied to a suitor's love letter (this lasted 10 minutes).

The Picturedrome made a point of including serials from the start because *Our Navy* began the second week of opening and continued for the next 8 weeks. The cinema had the sole rights for Luton on this film. The main feature shown in conjunction with part 4 was *A Prisoner Of War*, which was produced by Edison and depicted the last days of Napoleon on St Helena.

The cinema closed in October 1937, after showing *Pick A Star*, a Hal Roach production featuring Laurel and Hardy. It was reopened for a while and renamed the

Plaza, before finally closing. It became a warehouse, demolished in 1979. Successive owners were General Theatre Corporation, Southan Morris Circuit by 1929, leased to Union Cinema Co by 1936. It seated 550.

The Savoy Cinema, 51 George Street, opened on the 17 October 1938, in the same week as the Odeon. There was no grand opening in this case. Seating about 2,000, it was built by ABC Cinemas on land leased for a long period from Luton corporation. It was later renamed the **ABC** and is still open housing three separate cinemas in the one building. The editorial in the *Luton News* said that the lighting and effects could not be bettered in Luton. The comfort, legroom, silence and warmth, were second to none.

The first film was *Test Pilot* starring Spencer Tracy and Clark Gable.

The second film was *Woman against Woman* starring Herbert Marshall and Virginia Bruce; with Edgar Wallace's best seller *The Terror*, as second feature.

The price to get in had not gone up much since the early days of cinemas as 6d, bought entry to the stalls and 1s to the circle up to 4 pm, while in the evening the prices were 6d, 1s in the stalls and 1s 6d and 2s in the circle.

In an attempt to maintain audiences in 1948, midnight matinées were introduced, and at one, Spencer Tracy, Lana Turner and Zachary Scott starred in *Cass Timberlaine*. Cinemascope came in 1954 with its wide curved and inclined screen, which was first used on the 10th May.

The Union. 16–42 Gordon Street. There was a Grand Gala opening for the Union on 11 October 1937. It was opened by Robert Douglas, a famous British film star, who later turned to TV Production in Hollywood. Such crowds turned up that the police had difficulty in controlling them. Other film stars and the local member of parliament also attended. The cinema was owned by Union Cinemas Limited, and later by ABC Limited, who renamed it the **Ritz,** In July 1949 and it seated 2,400.

The opening programme was a mixture of film and variety with the film *Our Fighting Navy*, which starred Robert Douglas and was produced by Herbert Wilcox in May 1937. It told how a British ship saved the consul's daughter from a South American revolutionary battleship. On the stage were Terry's famous juveniles and 30 other artistes in a complete review. Luton's own version of *In Town Tonight* was also included. The BBC organist H. Robinson Cleaver, played the mighty Wurlitzer organ.

XXI The Union, Luton.

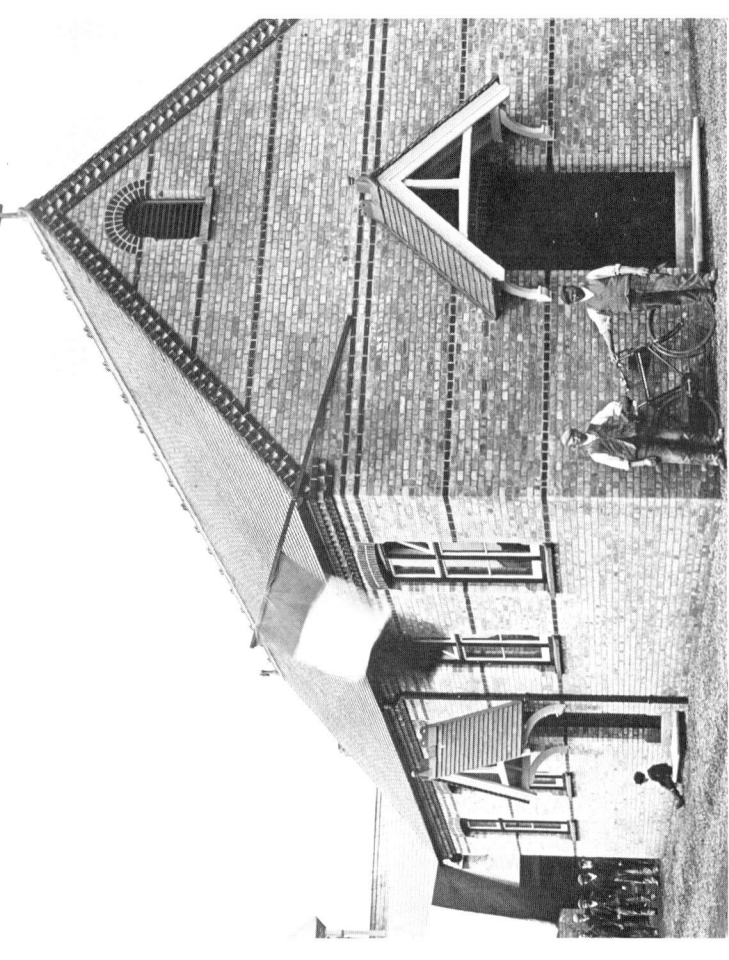

XXII   *The Parish Room, Potton, formerly Randall's Cinema.*

Children were not forgotten as they had their own Union Chums Club before the war.

3D first appeared in Luton, here, in 1954. The cinema finally closed in 1972, and is now Sand's Night Club.

The Wellington, 61 Wellington Street. This was formerly owned by the County Picture Theatre Proprietory Limited, who sold it in 1951 to Coronet Cinemas Limited. They renamed the cinema the **Coronet.** It had 450 seats.

The Wellington opened in May 1912, on the site of a former pub, *The Lamb,* and finally closed in May 1952. After being pulled down a new ring road was built across the site.

An early programme featured *The Peril, A Western Tramp,* and *Was He Justified?,* a film of 1,095 feet, that depicted a cleric hiding an evicted inventor who had blown up his landlord to avenge his wife's death. The pianist who accompanied the silent films was said to have only two tunes 'The Rustle of Spring' and 'Teddy Bears Picnic'.

The programme starting the 22 April 1938, was Ralph Lynn in *Up to the Neck,* a comedy produced by Herbert Wilcox in 1933, but reissued in 1937. The film tells how a bank clerk wants to become an actor and takes lessons at the local academy where he makes an enemy of the star pupil. When he inherits a fortune, he is asked to finance a play in which the enemy stars. After a quarrel between the two, Ralph Lynn takes over on the opening night despite being a very poor actor. He has to turn the play into burlesque to become successful. Lynn plays Norman B. Good, the hero.

The theatre seated about 400 people and used British Acoustic Films Limited, sound. It seems to have had two programmes each week for its whole life. Towards the end of the cinema's life, it showed only newsreels and cartoons.

WELLINGTON

TO-NIGHT, FRIDAY & SATURDAY—
THE COLD CURE
Featuring QUEENIE THOMAS & Star Cast, in a thrilling and exciting Comedy-Drama.

NEXT MONDAY—
KNORLOCK'S ATTRACTIONS
SOUTH of the EQUATOR
Featuring KENNETH McDONALD. An exciting Comedy-Drama. Also
WHAT PRICE LOVING CUP?
Starring VIOLET HOPSON & JAMES KNIGHT. Another of the thrilling Racing Series.

SERIAL, COMEDY, INTEREST & PATHE SUPER GAZETTE.

Potton

In 1937 there was a proposal made by the Cox Cinema Company to build a 400 seat cinema in a corner of the market square that had formerly been occupied by Messrs Valentine's the drapers. But it was never built.

Randall's Cinema, Brook End. This is an example of the local village hall being used to show films. It had only a short life in the late 1950s and finally closed in 1961. The Licensee Mr G. Randall showed 16 mm films in the cinema and must have taken a keen interest in the industry because he ran other local cinemas for brief periods. He sometimes included his own film in the newsreel to add local colour. Events such as the erection of the gas holder, weddings and scout parades were featured. The building was later used for industrial purposes.

Sandy

The Victory, Bedford Road, was opened in 1920 by Edward Charles Gray, in what had been the Youth Hall. That July the film *Belle of New York* was shown. Sandy String Band played for the films, the members being – Mr T. Hunt, cornet; Mr J. Hunt, flute; Mr Pentelow, violin; Mr J. Kemp, bass; and Mrs Ida Warren, piano. One notable film they accompanied was *Ben Hur*. Later Mrs Warren accompanied the films alone. Her successor who played 'requests' was Miss Gwen Marshall.

One evening there was consternation among the audience when it was announced that an episode of *The Red Glove* failed to arrive. The regulars were greatly upset as they had walked from the nearby villages to attend. The projector at the Victory was powered by a gas engine housed in an iron shed next to the building. It had a distinctive rhythmic sound, which could not be ignored.

Arthur Hill of Biggleswade, bought the Victory in 1928 and ran the cinema until the Cox Cinema Company bought it. The building suffered a fire in 1948, after which it had to be rebuilt incorporating a concrete floor of a building that also housed Sandy

XXIII The Victory, Sandy.

Liberal Club. The two had to be made independent, and the cinema exits could not be through the Club. 329 people could be seated with two of them on a small balcony. There were always problems with safety and the Liberal Club having to remove open fires for that reason.

When the Victory was reopened following the fire, in July 1950, it was renamed the **Albany** after the new owners home address in Bedford. The first film then was *Trotty True*, which featured Jean Kent. The new owners announced that they hoped to film local events for inclusion in their newsreels. The enterprise was not very successful, so it was taken over by George Randall of Potton, who re-equipped it. He aimed to show one programme on Monday and Tuesday, an 'X' film on Wednesday, and yet another programme the rest of the week. Gaumont Kalee projection equipment and cinemascope were introduced to show the film *Bhowani Junction*, in which Ava Gardner and Stewart Granger appeared. The reopening ceremony was performed by Lana Morris, and the collection taken at the time raised about £45 for Sandy Peace Memorial Fund.

The cinema in Sandy died a lingering death in February 1964. However, in 1967 it was specially licensed to show scouting films using hired equipment. Sandy Film Society also used the building for a time in 1968.

The room is now used by the 'Roundabout Club'.

Sharnbrook

The Midland Cinema This picture house has appeared in Kelly's Directory for Bedfordshire 1936 but enquiries made of local inhabitants have brought no further information. It may have been the Church Room which had a licence from the Stage Plays Performance Committee of the County Council for many years.

Shefford

There seems to have been a small cinema in Shefford for about ten years in the 1920s, possibly called the **Empire**, or the **New Hall Cinema**, South Bridge Street. Over most of the period there was a different licensee each year. In November 1920 Mr G. H. Borwell was refused permission to open on Christmas Day, as was Captain W. Grieve in 1923. One former resident remembers a weekly visit of a travelling

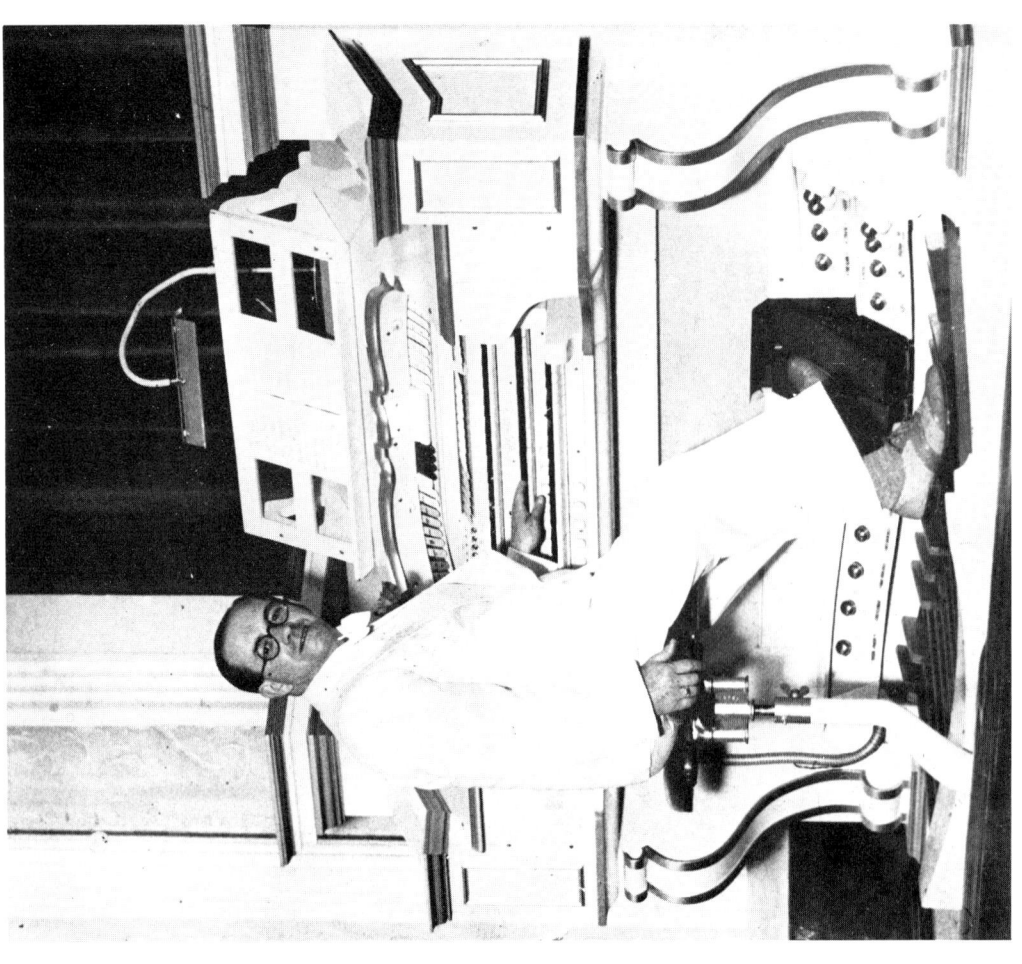

XXIV   Harold Ramsey. The Regent Cinema, Stotfold.

cinema that was held in a hut near the river Hit. The cinema was just off the Ampthill Road and stood against the slaughterhouse owned by King's the butchers. The power supply came from a huge tractor engine in the yard. This was so noisy it made the pianist play very loudly to accompany the silent films. The building was burnt down during the war when it was being used as the canteen for a Jewish School that had been evacuated to Shefford.

Stotfold

The first cinema in Stotfold was part of an iron warehouse owned by a haulage firm. The owner, Frank W. Smith, had his first application for a licence refused in September 1929. He was informed that he would get one if a fireproof wall was erected on the side next to the haulage firm. There were to be no doorways in the wall, except one near the stage, to enable scenery to be removed, and that the doorways on the other side were to meet the requirements of the County Surveyor. The 300 seat cinema was open every night and was filled to capacity from when it was opened on the 11 November 1929 to when it was replaced by **The Regent Cinema,** Regent Street, which was built especially to meet the increased demand. The Regent opened on the 15 April 1938 and was sold by the Smith family to the Central Cinema (South Norwood) Limited in 1948. The new cinema could seat about 700 people, so was really too big for Stotfold. In the early years the cinema was run as a family concern with them doing one job in the daytime before going in to show films in the evening. It cost £12,000 to build, and had a fully equipped stage and orchestra pit, an eight Rank Wurlitzer organ, and a room that was intended as a café over the entrance but was never used due to wartime restrictions. The regular organist was Harold Ramsey, but guests were also invited to play.

One film that was brought back several times was *Snow White and the Seven Dwarfs.* During the war the Pioneer Corps Orchestra came from Radwell, Herts, to play on Sunday evenings. There were also regular inter-denominational services of thanksgiving held in the cinema with the Salvation Army band playing. In 1949 the local Royal Air Force Association arranged a Battle of Britain concert at the Regent.

Despite the representatives of all the big film companies seeking to book their films into the Regent, it had to close in May 1952 due to lack of custom. It is now a Social Club.

Toddington

The Picturedrome, Gas Street, later renamed **The Cozy,** and again **The Rex.** This cinema was opened in September 1925 in the former Guides Hall. There was a gallery with double seats from which there were two exits down narrow winding wooden stairs. The cinema seated about 140 people. An early proprietor was J. H. W. Marsden who sold it to the Touring Talkie Picture Company by 1940. They sold it to the Midland and General Circuit Company Limited of Dunstable about 1952. The cinema was very small and only catered for local villagers. There were once nightly shows in 1940, using Imperial Sound equipment. The stage was 18 feet deep and with a width of 18 feet, and had one dressing room. Primitive sanitary arrangements were causing concern in 1952, and had to be replaced with new toilets and sewers. At the same time more compact projection equipment gave a better working space in the projection room. A stationary engine supplied the power, when it was not breaking down. Difficulties remained with safety aspects of the building and it remained unlicensed for a time, being reopened in January 1954. There were soon reports of damaged furniture and unsafe ceiling, made to the County Council. It finally closed in 1958 when L. N. Bryant was manager. Mr Bryant had formerly been the manager of the Cosy Cinema, Arlesey.

XXV   *The Picturedrome, Toddington, later renamed The Cozy.*